BY GOD'S GRACE ALONE

BY GOD'S GRACE ALONE

An easier-to-read and abridged version of
the classic "The Reign of Grace" by
Abraham Booth, first published
in 1768.

Prepared by H.J. Appleby

General editor J.K. Davies, B.D., Th.D.

© GRACE PUBLICATIONS TRUST
139 Grosvenor Avenue,
London, N5 2NH.
England.

1983

ISBN 0 946462 01 1

Distributed by: EVANGELICAL PRESS
16-18 High Street, Welwyn,
Hertfordshire, AL6 9EQ,
England.

Typeset in Great Britain by Berea Press,
Edinburgh, and printed in the USA.

Cover design — Helichrysum (Everlasting
flower) sometimes called Immortelle,
by John Shakespeare.
Name derived from the Greek Helios-
Chrusos, meaning 'sun gold'.

Contents

Abraham Booth's preface to the 16th and last edition of his book "The Reign of Grace", first published in 1768

I do not need to defend my writing of this book. If the truths in it are biblical, public disapproval of them will not worry me; if they are unbiblical, *no* defence could ever justify them!

I have tried not only to state the teachings of the gospel in a theoretical way but also to point out their practical value in a Christian's experience.

As a young man, I greatly opposed the truth of election. I realise now that was an attack on the sovereignty of God. So I think it my duty in this edition to explain how election completes the harmony of all the other truths of the gospel. (See chapter 3).

I am fully persuaded that the truths of sovereign grace — far from making people spiritually careless — are really for the comfort and holiness of sinful[1] men and women! If I were not so persuaded, I would never speak or write of these truths again.

May God bless you as you read these chapters. Then the work will have been of some use for God's glory.

A. BOOTH

Introduction

Paul and the early Christians were frequently attacked for their preaching by the religious Jews of their day. Was this because those Christians were living immoral lives? Indeed not! Was it because those Christians failed to do good works? No! Why then were they so persecuted? It was because the truth they preached was offensive to human pride.

They preached that salvation, even for the best person on earth, was only possible because of God's grace shown in Christ's death on the cross. They knew nothing of the requirement of human decision, which many today insist is necessary if a person is to be acceptable to God. They knew only one way of salvation — that of God being gracious. And this teaching of grace does not appear briefly in their preaching; it shines, reigns, triumphs; it is the *only* thing they preached. To them, any idea of human worthiness to be saved was totally wrong. Our most shining deeds and valuable qualities — while highly useful and right in our human circles — count for nothing in the matter of salvation. The apostolic preaching addressed all men as guilty, condemned, perishing wretches in God's sight. The only hope of salvation is *if* God will be gracious.

This teaching offends many people. Decent, moral people feel the need to defend what they call holy living

9

(though often more by talking about it than by doing it). They accuse this teaching of being likely to produce all manner of immoral living.

Nor is it merely that this preaching offends human pride by insisting that there cannot be any human worthiness for salvation. The preaching also offends because it insists that God being gracious is the only way of salvation, so that all who reject this teaching are necessarily left under an everlasting curse. This, it is said, is so very narrow-minded. It is much more charitable, surely, to allow those who differ in their sentiments to be safe in their own way? Paul, however, speaking about the gospel of grace, said emphatically: "If we, or an angel from heaven, should preach any gospel to you other than what we have preached to you, let him be accursed" (Galatians 1:8).

The preaching of the early church was an unceremonious message! It paid no respect to human worthiness. Its business was with the worthless and the miserable, whoever they were. It had nothing for those who were pleased with their own self-sufficiency. This was why Paul was so often attacked by the proud religious authorities of his day.

And this is still the basic difference between Biblical Protestantism and Roman Catholicism. As long as pride in his achievements infects the heart of a man, he will object to the doctrine of the apostles, not understanding its real nature. But wherever the gospel of grace has been modified, to allow some merit in human actions towards salvation, instead of holiness being promoted, the reverse has been true.

While self-sufficient people may despise a salvation which is only by God being gracious, the "poor in spirit" will love it! To the sensible sinner[1] the gospel of grace is a

10

joyful sound. And whereas those ignorant of this gospel are ready to imagine it will produce careless living, in fact we state boldly that it makes men holy.

True, some who hold this truth of salvation by grace merely in a theoretical way may live carelessly. They have never experienced the beauty of this gospel in their affections nor the power of it in their wills. So I write to show the power, glory and majesty of this gospel in the salvation of sinners. I shall try to illustrate the words of Paul: "EVEN SO GRACE MIGHT REIGN THROUGH RIGHTEOUSNESS TO ETERNAL LIFE THROUGH JESUS CHRIST OUR LORD" (Romans 5:21). And while I pray for spiritual wisdom to write truthfully, I entreat you to think carefully about the contents of the following pages.

1.
What is grace?

Paul uses the word "grace" to mean the opposite of "works and worthiness": "by grace you have been saved *not of works*" (Ephesians 2:8,9). "Grace" means undeserved kindness, or favour given *without it being earned in any way*.

By the word "mercy" we understand that someone who is in difficulty or in defeat is receiving a kindness. "Mercy " implies a suffering person to whom it is shown. Similarly, "grace" always presupposes unworthiness in the person receiving it. If anyone gives us anything by grace, it is because we do not deserve it. Anything we deserve, as of right, cannot be ours by grace. Grace and worthiness cannot be connected in the same act. They are as much opposites as are light and darkness. "If by grace, then it is no longer of works; otherwise grace is no longer grace" (Romans 11:6).

So we say we receive God's grace. We are by that also saying we are unworthy of it and cannot work for it. So we define "grace" as used in the New Testament, to be:

> The eternal and absolutely free favour of God shown by his giving spiritual and eternal blessings to guilty and unworthy persons.

In the following pages I shall try to describe what these spiritual and eternal blessings are. But for now, notice that God's grace is eternal.

Grace is not in any way dependent on human worthiness. It depends solely on God's will — not earned by merit, nor lost by guilt. Grace is absolutely free of any human influence. Therefore there is nothing that can defeat it once it is given. So God can say: "I have loved you with an *everlasting* love" (Jeremiah 31:3). Such is the glorious basis of our salvation.

Grace is not like a fringe of gold bordering a garment; not like embroidery, decorating a robe; but like the mercy-seat of the Tabernacle which was gold — pure gold — all gold, throughout. Therefore we learn how those who suggest that God's grace may be earned by good works are seriously deceived. God's grace refuses to be assisted in what it has to do. Does it not insult the sovereign God to suggest he needs the poor performances of people to help him? Grace is either absolutely free of all influence by us — or it is not grace at all.

2.
Salvation, all of grace!

"Grace reigns" says Paul in our text (Romans 5:21). So grace is compared to a king. In previous verses, sin is also compared to a king. As sin appears armed with destructive power, inflicting death, so grace appears armed with invincible power, lovingly determined to save. And where sin increased, grace increased all the more (verse 20). So grace is in control.

In other words, those whom God saves by his gracious will are certainly and completely saved. If God graciously rescues people from the power of sin and gives them new spiritual abilities, they will not then be left to make themselves holy enough for heaven. If God's gracious work were restricted in this way, the final outcome would still be in doubt. Grace would not be in control. Moreover, (assuming such a thing was possible), those who did make themselves holy by their own efforts would be so proud of what they'd done — which is the very opposite of grace!

If grace is to reign, therefore, it must be the sole means of salvation. By his gracious will, God must not only begin but also continue, and complete, the sinner's salvation. Then it can be certainly said that "grace reigns". Surely such a wonderful certainty glorifies God?

And grace suits our need better than anything else.

15

Since sin is such a tyrant to reign over us and to bring us to eternal death, what hope have we of salvation by our own efforts? When our consciences are alarmed by our many shameful failures, do we not begin to despair? But remember, salvation is by God's grace! The grace of God is based on the perfect and well-deserving obedience of Christ. Sin cannot destroy the value of that. So grace can reign over the greatest unworthiness. Indeed, it is only the unworthy with whom grace is at all concerned. This is amazing! This is delightful! There can be hope for the worst character if salvation is by the richness of reigning grace.

Having tried to show that grace reigns in salvation in general, I shall, in the following chapters, show particularly how grace reigns in our election — calling — pardon — justification — adoption — sanctification and perseverance.

3.
Part I, Election, or distinguishing grace[1]

God is glorious because he is perfect. All that he does is perfect. We must therefore say that even though the world about us, and the people in it, is now sadly affected by sin, there must still be some way in which God's glory can be established in it. To dispute this is to deny that everything God does comes to perfection and suggests that God was unable to stop the world developing as it has.

God created Adam and gave him freedom of choice, though knowing that he would sin and bring the whole human race under God's curse. If everything God does is perfect, then this happening, too, must be part of a process that will demonstrate the glorious perfection of God. Scripture teaches that by graciously choosing to save, gloriously, a vast family from the fallen race of Adam, God shows his limitless perfection. This act of God's gracious choice is commonly called election, or, distinguishing grace.

Election is a truth now much attacked. Without doubt it was thought a very important truth in the past, especially by the Reformers. But now (i.e. in Abraham Booth's day — Ed.) it is said to be offensive to human reason, immoral, damaging to true piety and hurtful to mankind at large. No wonder the truth is unpopular!

But why is this truth so attacked? Unless I am greatly mistaken, it is because it cuts away our human pride. By making salvation arise wholly from God's gracious decision, election leaves no difference between one person and another, as to why this person should be saved and not that one. God alone receives the glory for saving people. And the proud independence of human hearts resents that fact. There are other reasons, too, why this truth is attacked. But this reason is enough, for it is not my purpose here to argue in defence of election. Others, with more leisure and ability than I, have already done that very well. I shall simply explain what the truth means and how it helps us.

Since the scriptures speak of "the elect", it follows that not all the human race is included in that term. Where any are chosen, others must be refused. That is plainly implied by the words "elect" and "choose".

Those called "the elect" in scripture are not whole nations or communities, but individuals. They are described as having their names "written in heaven" (Luke 10:20) and "in the book of life" (Revelation 20:15). They are said to be "as many as were ordained to eternal life" (Acts 13:48). From these verses, we must conclude that the elect are particular persons.

This is also confirmed by the fact that salvation was obtained by Jesus Christ who became a mediator and substitute for those sinners. It is absurd to suppose anyone can be a substitute — or a mediator — for unknown persons. If one man becomes legally responsible for the debts of another, he will surely have exact knowledge of that particular person!

The salvation of anyone can only be certain if that person is precisely identified. Suppose it had simply been God's purpose to save "all who should believe in Jesus", then it would have remained doubtful whether any would ever actually be saved, because it would be uncertain whether any would believe.

But if you say, certainly some would believe; I reply, such certainty must arise from the purpose of God. There is no other way that the future can be certain. And if God did plan that some should believe, he must know who they are because their faith is "the gift of God" (Ephesians 2:8). Also, it seems clear that God always knew who would be saved, since several scriptures indicate that believers were chosen "before the foundation of the world" (Ephesians 1:4).

Is it possible to find any reason why the elect were chosen and others were left? No reason can be found in the individuals themselves, for all mankind is equally unworthy of receiving God's blessing. The only reason for making the difference between individuals is given by scripture. God said "I will have mercy on whom I will have mercy and I will have compassion on whom I will have compassion" (Romans 9:15).

Even though there was no difference originally between individuals, could it be that God *fore*saw those who would believe and therefore chose them? Not at all! For then grace would not reign, but would depend on people's faith.

Scripture shows that faith is not the cause, but the result, of being elect. "As many as had been appointed to eternal life believed" (Acts 13:48). "He chose us . . . that we should be holy" (Ephesians 1:4). "Whom he predestined, these he also called" (Romans 8:30). "You do not believe, because you are not of my sheep" (John 10:26). "God . . . has called us . . . not according to our works, but according to his own purpose . . . before time began" (II Timothy 1:9).

Faith, and holiness, are like twigs and branches, compared with the root of a plant. They are not themselves the root, nor the fruit; not the cause, nor the consummation. They are the result of the root growing and the means towards the fruit forming. So, faith and holiness are the result of grace and the means of reaching glory. "By grace you have been saved through faith" (Ephesians 2:8). Faith is not the cause, but the result of, election.

Besides all this, if people were elected because God saw they would believe, why need they then be elected? Those who have faith must be saved, anyway! If faith is there already, election is unnecessary! But scripture insists, in many places, on the fact of election.

Paul explains the matter for us most plainly in Romans 9:10-23. He also answers supposed objections raised against election, by insisting that if God be God, he must have the right to do what he wishes. If human kings are allowed to do what they like, must God — who rules over all things — be denied royal rights?

God's supreme perfection means that he cannot make unwise decisions, or govern unjustly; or plan without love. So, after carefully examining the sovereignty of God, Paul exclaims: "Oh, the depth of the riches both of the wisdom and knowledge of God!" (Romans 11:33). Whatever God does, he does as a wise and compassionate Father. Why did he choose to save any, when all are undeserving? Because our Maker is merciful! Why choose some and not others? Because our Maker has indisputable right to do what he wishes with his own.

Now I want to consider what God intended to achieve by his use of distinguishing grace. We too easily assume that all God is concerned about is the happiness of the elect and the tormenting of sinners. This is a great mistake. It is blasphemous to suggest that a supremely good God takes delight in the misery of tormented sinners.

The Bible clearly states that the reason for God's acting in grace is the praise of his own glory. When God punishes a sinner, God shows how much his pure nature is opposed to sin. When God saves sinners from what they deserve, he shows his amazing and gracious mercy. All God's acts, therefore, display some aspect of his glory. God's acts are done so "that he might make known the riches of his glory" (Romans 9:23).

So God does what he does in order to show his glory. And not only that. The ways in which God does things also display how glorious he is. The salvation of sinners is brought about by the life, death and resurrection of Jesus Christ, the eternal Son of God; and by the Holy Spirit working in the lives of believers, thus making it possible for them to be holy. All these acts of God are glorious!

Also, what God does is unchangeable. This demonstrates his glory. How? If he can change his mind, it must be for better or worse. If for the better, then he was not perfectly wise before. If for the worse, then he is not wise now. So, the fact that God never needs to change his mind, is another evidence of his glorious perfection. He *is* always right, never needing to change. "Whom he predestined . . . these he also glorified" (Romans 8:30). If God could change his mind, Paul would not be so certain as that! But since God's electing those whom he will save is said in the Bible to be unchangeable, we know that it must also be gloriously right.

Part II, Election promotes holiness

Since God's election of his people is taught in the scriptures, we expect it to contribute to the believer's holiness.

Humility, love and gratitude are three essential elements in true religion. The Bible teaching of election promotes all three.

Distinguishing grace certainly promotes humility. All people are equally ruined. Sinners are not saved because of their worthiness, but only because of God's gracious choice of them. So none has any reason to be proud. Salvation is never "of works, lest anyone should boast" (Ephesians 2:9). So distinguishing grace humbles believers. They are forced to acknowledge they have no more right to be saved than the greatest wretch who is already in hell. As Paul wrote: "Who makes you differ from another? And what do you have that you did not receive? Now if you did indeed receive it, why do you glory as if you had not received it?" (I Corinthians 4:7).

Moreover, God's election of his children creates in them a great love for him. When they realise all the blessings of salvation that God has graciously given them, though they did not deserve them any more than anyone else, they must be full of amazed love! God might justly have sent them to hell, but has lifted them to heaven instead. Will they not love him for that?

And that love will express itself in gratitude. If God has done so much for us without our deserving it, should not we give ourselves wholly to him in thankful service? With Paul we say: "Blessed be the God and Father of our Lord Jesus Christ, who has blessed us with every spiritual blessing in the heavenly places in Christ, just as he chose us in him before the foundation of the world, that we should be holy and without blame before him in love" (Ephesians 1:3,4).

Humility towards our fellows, love and gratitude to God — these are the fruits of an understanding of distinguishing grace. Election, therefore, influences us to become better believers.

But however helpful this truth may be to those who are already believers, will it not discourage enquirers? Those who are seeking to become believers might argue: "If I am not among God's elect, then no matter how much I desire to be saved, I cannot be".

This may seem a plausible argument; in fact, it is a great mistake. Let me illustrate the matter. Suppose food is suddenly presented to a very hungry man. Would it be sensible for him to argue: "I do not know if God intends me to be nourished by this particular food. Therefore, no matter how much I want it, I cannot have it". Would it not be far more sensible to say: "I have a healthy appetite. Food is the means of satisfying that appetite. Therefore I will eat this food".

Now Christ is the bread of life, the food of our souls. This heavenly food is provided by grace, exhibited in the gospel, and freely presented without exception to all that hunger. What, then, has the spiritually awakened sinner to do but, as the Lord enables him, to take, eat and live for ever. Sinners are not encouraged to believe in Jesus on the grounds of knowing they are elected. No, the news of God's mercy is addressed to sinners *considered as ready to perish.* All, without exception, who know their danger and feel their want, are invited at once to receive spiritual blessings, before ever they think about their election. So this truth need not frighten an enquirer or any person who is conscious of their sin. Those who are unconcerned about their souls, or have a high opinion of their own goodness, will not bother with election, anyway!

But may it not be argued: "If I am among the elect, then I will be saved, no matter how I behave." So doesn't this scriptural teaching of distinguishing grace encourage a believer to be careless?

Sometimes you may find people who profess to believe in election and whose lives are unholy. But such people are deceiving themselves. Election does not merely mean that a certain number of persons will certainly arrive in heaven. The reason for election is that God's people "should be holy and without blame before him" (Ephesians 1:4): i.e. election means that a certain number of *holy* persons reach heaven.

God has not merely appointed the end (heaven) to which the elect will come; but has also appointed the way by which they shall come there. Paul writes: "God from the beginning chose you for salvation through sanctification by the Spirit and belief in the truth" (II Thessalonians 2:13). So, an essential part of the spiritual experience of elect persons must be "sanctification" and "belief in the truth". Where these are not present, there is no election.

There is another argument, similar to this last one, which is sometimes raised against the truth of election. It is said: "What is the use of preaching, praying, and self-denial? If the elect are already certainly chosen, there is no need of these things". The answer to the previous argument is also an answer to this one: i.e. God deliberately uses preaching, praying and self-denial to bring about that very holy living for which he chose his people. I can show the absurdity of this argument by another illustration.

Let us agree that there is a God who governs all our human affairs by his providence. If God has planned everything that he will do, the objection that "if one is elect then one need not be holy" also applies to all the affairs of daily life. If God has planned all human affairs, then whether we are well or ill; whether we succeed or fail in our trade; whether we are skilled or not in our work, are all governed by providence. But who is so absurd as to argue: "It doesn't matter whether I eat, or sleep, or study, since the circumstances of my life are already settled by providence!" Since we don't argue so absurdly in relation to the affairs of our natural life, why argue so in relation to the affairs of our spiritual life?

God's perfect knowledge includes all the details of our lives, as well as our ultimate end. We cannot separate the details from the end. God foresees only those in heaven whom he foresees are made holy by daily spiritual effort; and he foresees none in hell except those sinners who daily reject his truth.

"But", some argue further, "this teaching makes God unjust, since he is gracious to some and not to all. God has become unfair". I answer: injustice can only be present where reward which is due in some matter *is not given.* If a magistrate applies the law strictly in the case of poor people but leniently for the rich, he *is* unjust. But if, as a benefactor, he is generous to those in need among his neighbours, we never argue that he is obliged to be generous to *everyone in need.* That would be impertinent of us! If it is a matter of gracious giving, there cannot be injustice even though all do not receive. And this is even more true with God, because he is the Creator who has absolute right to do what he wishes with his own — and his perfect nature means that nothing he does will be wrong.

Let me ask you whether all people have sinned, or not? If they have, then every person is guilty before God. If that is admitted, then even if all perish, God must be just. And the election of some to be saved does not harm the non-elect. Non-election is not an unjust punishment. To suggest that God must not leave any unsaved is to imply that all people have a right to salvation. But no-one has such a right. Salvation is purely by grace.

The truth is that the argument "God is unjust in electing some and not all" arises from the high opinions we (wrongly!) form of ourselves and the too small view we have of God. Must the high and lofty one be so bound that he cannot do as he pleases?

Let me show you now the real and practical value for us of election. First, the truth has something to say to the careless sinner. You have seen that all are guilty in God's sight and that he has chosen some to salvation, leaving others to the just consequences of their sins. How do you know that this is not *your case?* To be rejected of God is to be lost for ever. Are you still unconcerned? You are in the hands of an offended God and yet have no certain idea what he will do with you! If you do fear the possibility of hell, you know it is exactly what you deserve. You have good reason to tremble. Meditate on these awful facts! May the Lord enable you to "flee from the coming wrath" (Matthew 3:7). So from this, it is clear that to teach that God's love is general and equal to all mankind, and that Christ died for all, can lull consciences to sleep. If all are equally loved and saved, why need I worry? Only the scripture truths of distinguishing grace and Christ as the substitute for his people alone, have the ability to arouse the careless sinner.

Second, the truth of distinguishing grace has something to say to the believer. Are you a *true* believer? Then this truth shows you whom to praise for that and tells you to be humble! And this truth also assures you that all who receive this grace are secure for eternity, for nothing can overthrow God's grace. It reigns! How important, then, "to make your calling and election sure" (II Peter 1:10). Are you persuaded that this truth of election is a Bible truth? Then make sure you enjoy all its benefits. Surely, among all the names which the people of God are given in the Bible, the name "elect of God" is the most remarkable. It signifies that you are authorised to enjoy all the immense privileges that grace gives. "A chosen generation, a royal priesthood, a holy nation, his

26

own special people, that you may proclaim the praises of him who called you out of darkness into his marvellous light" (I Peter 2:9).

Third, this truth of distinguishing grace has something to say to the nominal believer, who talks much about doctrine but in whose life unholiness, pride and malice are so often seen. Are you like that? Then you may talk as long as you please about the doctrine; it will do you no good. Your life makes plain that you are an enemy of grace. You are really obeying your sinful appetites. You don't really love God. May that grace of which you talk, without any experience of it, mercifully deliver you from sin. It would be hard to find a more pitiful case than a person who pretends to know what he doesn't actually experience.

4.
How grace controls our being called by by God

The fact that God graciously chose a people for himself out of the whole sinful human race is not at first known by the chosen ones. They know nothing of the matter before they are converted. The Holy Spirit must, therefore, actually call them individually, or they will never know they are God's children! This experience is described in scripture as being "called of God" (I Corinthians 1:9); "called by grace" (Galatians 1:15); and "called by the gospel" (II Thessalonians 2:14). The Holy Spirit uses the gospel to do this calling.

Sinners are spiritually dead. They welcome gospel truth only after the Holy Spirit makes them spiritually alive. "The dead will hear . . . and those who hear will live" (John 5:25). The newly awakened sinner may feel far off from God, but the gospel says: "The one who comes to me I will by no means cast out" (John 6:37). So, the spiritually alive sinner comes to Jesus, trusting the truth of the gospel. This, in brief, is the experience of being called by grace. The fact that any sinner is ever called is entirely due to divine grace. "God called me by his grace", said Paul. And no saint will suggest any other cause.

Sinners, generally, look on their offences against God

as failings rather than crimes. They sleep in their sin, dreaming of some general mercy to be shown to them. They lie unaware of their peril, until God's Spirit touches them to convince them of their sinfulness. But when they are aroused from that spiritual death by the Spirit of God, they suddenly learn that every one of their sins brings them under God's curse. The duties neglected, God's good gifts ungratefully used, the rebellious acts committed against God, crowd in on the newly-awakened mind and trouble the soul. Conscience sharpens her sting and guilt becomes a burden. God's holy law is seen to be just. Ruin is seen to be inevitable for unforgiven sinners.

Then, by the Spirit and the word of truth, awakened sinners also learn that they are unable to escape from God's law by any efforts of their own. This conviction makes them amazed at their former ignorance and indifference. Now they know the scriptures are true when they describe man's natural condition as a "dog returns to his own vomit", and, "a sow, having washed, to her wallowing in the mire" (II Peter 2:22); and an "open tomb" (Psalm 5:9). Instead of living every moment in uninterrupted and eager love of God, as the law requires, they have — Oh! the shame of it! — lived wholly in the love of themselves and of sin. Surely the sentence of God's law is just! "Cursed is everyone who does not continue in all things which are written in the book of the law, to do them" (Galatians 3:10). Since they have not so continued, they are indeed cursed.

Now it must be obvious that such persons[1] will readily admit that any hope for them at all must only be if God is gracious. Grace, as a way of salvation, is truly welcome to anyone who has learnt his unworthiness in God's sight.

You would think that a sinner awakened to his need would run to receive such gracious salvation. Wonderful truth! Astonishing favour! What more could I want? But observation shows that awakened sinners are sometimes very slow to receive this comfort. This is not because God's grace is defective, nor because the salvation is somehow incomplete. But often because the sinner fears that he has not yet felt the sense of his sin *enough;* or else because he does not feel he wants Christ enough. This is still to misunderstand the glory of salvation by grace.

Our conviction of sin, or wanting Christ to be our Saviour, do not persuade God to be gracious to us. They *are* necessary experiences for us to have, to make us willing to receive grace, but they are *not* necessary to make God be gracious to us. It is grace that controls God's call of us, not how much we sorrow for our sin or want to be saved. We must beware of wishing for the miseries of unbelief in order to get permission to believe.

The call of the gospel is to unhappy sinners who have nothing of their own on which to rely. The person who truly believes in Christ must rely on him as justifier of the ungodly (Romans 4:5). The sinner who feels somehow better than the ungodly is not encouraged to come to Christ — but the sinner who knows he is as guilty as all the rest! "I did not come to call the righteous", said Jesus, "but sinners, to repentance" (Matthew 9:13).

The basis of a believer's hope and the source of his spiritual joy are *not* thinking that he has done something to earn his own salvation (call it "believing", or what you will), *but* the truths that salvation is of grace and that the Saviour "has come to save that which was lost" (Matthew 18:11). A believer must depend on grace which requires no worthiness, and a Saviour who supplies all needed righteousness.

Realising, then, that he is in the same guilty condition as all other ungodly people in the world, the awakened sinner is convinced that his calling must only be because

30

God has been gracious. He knows no other reason to account for it. He is fully persuaded that God made the first move. As he thinks about his experience of being awakened to know his spiritual need, he says: "I am found by him whom I neither loved nor sought".

To be called of God is an act of God's grace alone. To realise that God's distinguishing grace has singled you out, and called you, though you were no different from every other sinner, must fill your heart with Christian gratitude. It will fill you with a great incentive to godly obedience and eager Christian service.

What shall I say to you who are as yet uncalled? If you leave this world as you are now, you are lost for ever. Only those who are called here are glorified hereafter. Do not suppose that a knowledge of the facts of the gospel will save you, if your heart is cool and has no feeling of love for God. What advantage is it to leave a memory of a respectable character among your friends if you yourself are damned? God grant this may not be the case with my readers!

5.
God's pardon for our sin comes because God is gracious

Pardon for sin is something the spiritually awakened sinner most longs for. But is pardon possible? Without the Bible, we should never know if such forgiveness was possible. We see, in scripture, that God does speak of his mercy from the earliest days: "The LORD . . . forgiving iniquity and transgression and sin" (Exodus 34:7).

God talks, in the Bible, about his forgiveness in many different ways, just as your human sinfulness is also described in many different ways. Sinners are described as "defiled" and "loathsome". God's pardon is described as "cleansing" and "covering". Sinners are described as "debtors" and as "burdened". Pardon is spoken of as "blotting out" debt and "lifting up" the downcast. "Scarlet" offences are made "whiter than snow". God's pardon is so suitable to your sin!

God's pardon for sin is free, full and everlasting[1]. These three things deserve more detailed consideration, to show how completely God graciously pardons sinners.

This pardon is free. There are no conditions to be fulfilled before it is given. Scripture examples make this clear. What conditions did Saul of Tarsus fulfil before he was pardoned? None whatever. He was an enemy of God. He received pardon, not because he fulfilled certain conditions but "that in me first Jesus Christ might show all long-suffering, as a pattern to those who are going to believe on him for everlasting life" (I Timothy 1:16). Saul though undeserving, was pardoned "as a pattern" for us of God's pardoning grace.

What conditions did Zaccheus, or the Samaritan woman, or the Philippian gaoler, fulfil to obtain pardon? None whatever! None deserved to be pardoned. And other instances could also be quoted, but I shall be content with only one more. What conditions did the dying thief perform in order to be pardoned? None whatever! He was a notorious sinner. Could he possibly have expected a happy answer to his prayer: "Remember me . . ."? His pardon was an act of divine grace alone. That *only* he was pardoned of the two thieves was an act of distinguishing grace (see chapter 3).[2]

Though this pardon is free to sinners, never forget that it was bought at great cost by Christ. Pardon for the least of our offences was only possible because he fulfilled the most dreadful conditions — his incarnation, his perfect obedience to divine law and his death on the cross. The pardon that is absolutely free to the sinner had a heavy cost for the Saviour.

Yet at the very moment of paying that cost, as though to show that it was not for persons who are righteous or worthy in their own eyes, the dying Jesus freely pardoned a thief. Clearly, pardon is by grace; and grace is favour given without prior conditions being fulfilled.

I think that enough facts have now been given to prove that pardon is free. I could easily add more. But I leave these out and only remind you of a remarkable verse: "When we were enemies we were reconciled to God through the death of his Son" (Romans 5:10). Plainly, then, pardon is not because of anything good these "enemies" have done!

Second, this pardon is full. Even one sin brings the curse of the law on a sinner. Pardon must be full enough to include every sin and must extend to the worst sins, however wicked they are, or it would be inadequate. A person with one sin left unpardoned, is damned.

The blood of Christ has infinite value because of the glorious dignity of him who shed it. Christ's death is able "to cleanse us from all unrighteousness" (I John 1:9), and that means from *each* sin — be it ever so evil; and from *all* sins — be they ever so numerous.

We may well cry out: "Who is a God like you, pardoning iniquity, and passing over the transgression of the remnant of his heritage? He does not retain his anger for ever, because he delights in mercy. He will again have compassion on us, and will subdue our iniquities. You will cast all our sins into the depths of the sea" (Micah 7:18,19).

Come, then, trembling sinner! Think about the riches of grace! Don't let one sin, nor a multitude of sins, make you despair. God never confers favour because of the worthiness of the sinner, and never withholds it because of unworthiness. Grace is free, and full. Rest on this!

Third, this pardon is everlasting. This is the crowning achievement of a complete pardon. It must be irreversible. And scripture speaks clearly: "Their sins and their lawless deeds I will remember no more" (Hebrews 8:12). This is not a conditional promise but an absolute one. It does not depend on the subsequent perfect behaviour of the sinner. (If it did, then that pardon would certainly fail to be kept.) It depends on the eternal value of the Lord's atoning death and the unshakeable faithfulness of God. "As far as the east is from the west, so far has he removed our transgressions from us" (Psalm 103:12). "Who shall bring a charge against God's elect?" (Romans 8:33). These strong experssions mean that the pardon can never be reversed.

The fact that God chastises his children when they sin does not mean that they can lose their pardon. Chastisement is an evidence of his love and concern for them, not a sign of his casting them off.

The fact that believers continually pray for forgiveness of sin does not mean that they are not already pardoned. They are praying for a *sense* of their pardon. We are not to imagine that, as often as they sin, repent, confess and seek forgiveness, God makes new acts of pardon. But they do need to realise again and again that the pardon is already theirs, as God's children.

How glorious, then, is this forgiveness which springs from God's grace. How complete the pardon is! There is nothing to discourage the most unworthy sinner applying for it. No-one has any reason to say: "Alas, my sins are too great".

"What shall we say then? Shall we continue in sin that grace may abound? Certainly not!" (Romans 6:1). Rather, the pardoned sinner will say, with the warmest gratitude: "Bless the Lord, O my soul; and all that is within me, bless his holy name! . . . who forgives all your iniquities . . . who redeems your life from destruction . . ." (Psalm 103:1,3).

"The forgiveness that is with God is such as becomes him. It is not like that narrow, difficult, half-hearted, with-strings-attached forgiveness, among men; but it is full, free, bottomless, boundless, absolute — such as becomes the excellencies of God. Remember this, poor souls, when you are to deal with God in this matter. Pardon is not merited by godly duties done before but is the strongest motive to live godly lives afterwards. He that will not receive pardon, unless he can one way or another deserve it, shall not

35

be a partaker of it. He that pretends to have received it, and does not find himself obliged to be obedient to God because of it, has not truly partaken of it!"[3]

Reader, is not such a pardon suitable for you? Are you longing to be forgiven? Then look to Jesus who died. What you so much long for is a free gift made possible because of his sacrifice on behalf of sinners.

Are you already pardoned? Then your heart should be full of holy love to the Lord and compassion towards any person who offends you. The person who pretends to be pardoned but does not forgive other people "is a liar" (I John 4:20).

6.
Part I — Our justification comes by grace (Proofs)

The doctrine of justification is how a sinner is accepted by a holy God. It is a most important truth. To make a mistake about it could have dangerous consequences. So this truth requires our serious thought.[1]

Justification is a legal term; it does not mean actually making a person righteous in nature. Justification is the act of a judge pronouncing a person not guilty. So justification is the opposite of condemnation. A sentence of condemnation is never supposed *to make* a person a criminal; it merely says, This person ought to be punished. So justification doesn't say that the person *is* holy, but that the person is to be *regarded as* deserving reward.

There are two possible ways for people to be justified. If a person could be found who never broke God's law, then that person would be justified *by the law*. But the Bible says: "all have sinned" (Romans 3:23); and "there is no-one who does good, no, not one" (Romans 3:10). Clearly, then, no-one will ever be justified by the law. So the Bible talks of a "righteousness of God apart from the law" (Romans 3:21). This is the justification which is by God's grace and is revealed in the gospel. We shall now consider this justification.

We are told that "it is God who justifies" (Romans 8:33).

But he is the very one whom we have offended by our sins. So this justification is certainly because God is gracious and not because we deserve it.

All three divine Persons of the Trinity have a part in justifying us. The Father designed the way it was done. He gave his Son to keep the law perfectly on behalf of sinners. The divine Son perfectly obeyed his Father's will and endured the curse of the law sinners broke. And the Holy Spirit reveals the free availability of the gospel to sinners and enables them to receive it. So, in the triumphant language of Paul, we may ask: "Who shall condemn?" If the Triune God justifies, who is greater than he, to dispute it?

The Bible says that the persons to whom this wonderful favour is granted are sinners and ungodly. This means that justification is "to him who does not work but believes on him who justifies the ungodly" (Romans 4:5).

> "This expression 'God who justifies the ungodly' causes some to respond, angrily, that such a doctrine will overthrow the need for holiness and good works. What need can there be for them, if God justifies the *un*godly? But the apostle does not say God justifies those who *continue* ungodly. All who are justified were, the moment before, ungodly. But all who are justified are, in that instant, made godly. We must insist the scripture says God justifies the ungodly. Since, it is said, the one justified 'does not work', then all his supposed worthiness is excluded from being the cause of his justification."[2]

Justification takes place only because God is gracious. This is expressed emphatically by the words "being justified freely by his grace" (Romans 3:24). If these

38

words do not prove that justification is entirely free, without the least regard to any supposed good in the sinner, then I do not know what words could prove that! We are plainly told that the blessing is *without any cause in us* — that is what "freely by grace" means.

There are no conditions to be fulfilled, no merit to be earned — either with or without God's help — no pre-requisites at all, for the sinner to be pronounced "not guilty". Nothing is required, except that God be gracious!

But how can a holy and just God apparently ignore the sinner's ungodliness and justify him? How can an unrighteous person be pronounced righteous? Isn't that a miscarriage of justice?

The righteousness by which anyone is to be justified in God's sight must be a perfect righteousness. God's law requires perfection and can accept no less. But where shall the sinner find such a perfection? "By the deeds of the law no flesh will be justified" (Romans 3:20). Far from the law of God justifying a sinner, it denounces him as the sinner he is! For as many as "rely on observing the law are under a curse" (Galatians 3:10). For he who shall "stumble in one point . . . is guilty of all" (James 2:10). So there is no perfect righteousness for the sinner this way!

If righteousness was possible by the keeping of God's law, Christ need not have come. If men could be justified by the excellence of their own lives, then "Christ died in vain" (Galatians 2:21). "Therefore we conclude", wrote Paul, "that a man is justified by faith apart from the deeds of the law" (Romans 3:28).

Our faith, however, is not the reason for our justification. Believers are said to be justified *by* faith, not *because of* faith. No man has perfect faith. If faith were the reason for justification, then some believers might be justified by a more perfect faith; others by a less perfect faith. Or else, some are more justified than others! All this is absurd. And it makes faith into a way of earning justification. No! The righteousness of God is said to be "revealed . . . to faith" (Romans 1:17). Faith therefore cannot be what makes us righteous.[3]

Nor are we accepted by God because of any holiness produced in us by the Holy Spirit, or because of good deeds we do with his help. If such holiness is thought of as being produced by ourselves, then it must be called our own righteousness. But the apostle Paul makes it plain that he greatly desires "to be found in Christ, not having my own righteousness" (Philippians 3:9).

If we say our own righteousness *is* the condition of our justification, then we are trying to earn our acceptance with God through human effort. We are putting ourselves back under the covenant of works; that is the opposite of the covenant of grace. The covenant of works was the arrangement God made with Adam, in which God required perfect personal obedience as the condition of life (Genesis 2:16,17).

The covenant of grace, however, is an arrangement whereby God makes promises of blessing to sinners without any conditions whatever; indeed, this covenant is actually called "the covenant of promise" (Ephesians 2:12).

If, then, the sinner seeking justification is ungodly; if the Supreme Governor of the world demands perfection of obedience; if such perfection cannot be found in our behaviour, nor even in our faith and good deeds; how shall we be justified? By a substitute who could perform all that is necessary and place it to the credit of our account! So we are said to be made righteous by the obedience of Christ (Romans 5:19) and to be "justified by his blood" (Romans 5:9). Our justification is by God's grace alone, because Christ's saving work is credited to us.

Part II — Our justification comes by grace (Examples)

The Bible makes it very clear that the believer is not justified by his own personal righteousness but by a righteousness given him by another. Christ obediently kept God's law perfectly. Our sins were atoned for by his death. We can be declared righteous because of the value of Christ's life and death on our behalf. God is satisfied that his laws are still preserved, unbroken; Christ kept them all.

This was the way God justified Abraham. Even though Abraham obeyed at once when called out of Ur (Genesis 12:1); even though he submitted at once to the command to sacrifice his only son Isaac (Genesis 22:2); even though he earned the name "the friend of God" (James 2:23); even though his obedience proved that his faith was genuine, and in that sense his deeds declared him to be righteous; yet none of those things were the reason for God accepting him. "For if Abraham was justified by works, he has something of which to boast" (Romans 4:2). But though he might perhaps be able to boast before his fellow men, he could not do so before God. What does the Bible say? "Abraham believed God and it was *accounted to him* for righteousness" (Romans 4:3). Paul goes on to speak immediately of one "who does not work but believes on him who justifies the ungodly" (Romans 4:5). Abraham is considered ungodly. Righteousness has *to be reckoned to him,* for he had none of his own.

We are told that the Bible was written "also for us. It (i.e. the work of the redeemer — Ed.) shall be imputed to us who believe" (Romans 4:24). So God uses the same method to justify believers to day as he did for Abraham then.

Paul also uses David as an example. Does David describe the blessed man as being justified because he kept God's laws perfectly? Not at all! Paul said: "David also describes the blessedness of the man to whom God imputes righteousness apart from works" (Romans 4:6). And, "Blessed is the man to whom the Lord shall not impute sin" (Romans 4:8).

Righteousness imputed; righteouness apart from the law; righteousness apart from works; this was the language of Paul. And this was what the early church believed. We are justified by God's grace alone.

Having seen what Paul says about Abraham and David, let us consider his own case, as he describes it in Philippians 3:4-9. Surely he makes it perfectly clear that no-one who is not perfectly righteous can be accepted by God. There are two kinds of righteousness — the one Paul calls "our own", which is by law-keeping; the other is "the righteousness of God", which is through faith in Christ. Paul says *he* was justified by God's grace alone.

There are many other passages of scripture which can be used to prove that justification is by grace; that it is imputed to sinners and never earned by them. I present you with just a few, as follows:

1. Believers are justified are ungodly. Their pardon cannot, therefore, be the result of their own goodness. Nor can it be the result of the supposed goodness of any other sinners who may even be justified believers. We humans cannot pass righteousness from one to another in that way. So justification can only be ours if the perfect and infinite righteousness of Christ can be reckoned to our account. This is called imputation.

2. In Romans 5:12-21, Paul speaks of our being ruined because of Adam's sin. He states (verse 14) that Adam was a type of the Messiah who was to come. The comparison between Adam and Christ is that just as

42

Adam's guilt is imputed to all his natural descendants, so the obedience of Christ is imputed to all his spiritual descendants. By the one, many were made sinners; by the other, many were made righteous. Imputation is the method in both cases.

3. Perhaps the truth for which I am arguing is most vividly shown in the following verse: God "made him who knew no sin to be sin for us, that we might become the righteousness of God in him" (II Corinthians 5:21). Now it is plain that Christ was not "made to be sin" by actually sinning. And he was certainly not punished for any sin of his own. The only way he could bear our sin was for it to be reckoned to be his, or, imputed to him. And since Paul says the same method is used in each half of this statement (II Corinthians 5:21), we may surely deduce that: as an innocent person can only be made sin by imputation, so a guilty person can only be made righteous by imputation. Or, as no criminal act of Christ's made him to be sin, so no holy activity of ours makes us righteous. We are not justified with our own righteousness. God graciously imputes it to us.

4. The objections against Paul's teaching make it quite clear that he preached that our good deeds are never the reason for our justification. Paul was accused of ignoring the divine commands and suggesting we do evil that good may come (Romans 3:8,31). Obviously, then, Paul was never understood to teach that we do *good* things to earn our justification, or those accusations would never have been made! Those who teach that good deeds are necessary to earn our justification are not likely to be accused of teaching that the law is *not* to be kept! (In reply to this attack, Paul made it plain that whereas good deeds are not the reason why the believer is justified, every justified believer will seek to do them).

5. The rightousness by which we are justified is called

"the gift of righteousness" which we "receive" (Romans 5:17). If believers receive it (i.e. if it is given them), then obviously they have not earned justification by doing righteous deeds. We don't *earn* gifts.

6. The purpose of the gospel is to reveal the righteousness of God (Romans 1:17); and to display the richness of God's grace, as the believer depends wholly on Jesus for salvation. The sinner dare not give any virtues as the reason for his justification, even if he possesses the meekness of Moses, the patience of Job, the zeal of Paul and the love of John. Our justification displays the glory of God.

It is sad to see people becoming weary as they try "to establish their own righteousness" (Romans 10:3). If you, my reader, despite all I have said, still feel you must rely on your obedience to please God, let me remind you of the nature of this God whom you seek to please. In his presence even holy angels veil their faces and cry "Holy, holy, holy". His eyes are as a flame of fire. He is jealous of his own glory. His anger is such that earth and heaven will flee from his face. What arguments, then, could *you* use, to recommend yourself to him?

Think of what some biblical saints said: "Though I were righteous, my own mouth would condemn me; though I were blameless, it would prove me perverse" (Job 9:20). "In your sight no-one living is righteous" (Psalm 143:2). "Woe is me, for I am ruined, because I am a man of unclean lips" (Isaiah 6:5).

So is it wise, can it be safe, for you to trust in your own imperfect deeds when saints such as Job, David and Isaiah talked like this? If their personal obedience to God would not bear his scrutiny better than this, how inferior your obedience must be! Better by far to have a righteousness which is perfect and an obedience which is divine, graciously given by God and freely available through faith!

7.
Our adoption comes by grace

God does not merely declare that believers are righteous (which is justification). He also adopts them as his children. The believer not only becomes a *friend* of God — though that is a great favour — but the believer also becomes an adopted *heir* of God, with indisputable right of inheritance.

In ancient Greece or Rome, it was the custom for a wealthy man who could have no children of his own, to choose someone from another family and publicly and legally make him his heir. Such a chosen person had not the slightest claim to be adopted in this way. But once the adoption was done, he no longer belonged to his former family. He was the rightful heir of his benefactor.

Notice how the benefits which God graciously gives the believer are growing in richness:

> when he pardons us, we become his friends;
> when he justifies us, we are declared righteous;
> when he adopts us, we are made heirs.

The Bible described believers as "children of God". This is because they are born of God, married to Christ, and adopted into the heavenly family. No wonder the apostle John exclaims: "See how great a love the Father has bestowed upon us, that we should be called 'children of God' " (I John 3:1).

These astonishing benefits are given, not because of any worthiness in believers but only because God wants to be gracious. He "predestined us to adoption as sons . . . according to the good pleasure of his will, to the praise of the glory of his grace" (Ephesians 1:5). The purpose God has in view, in adopting believers into his family, is that his grace should be praised.

Those whom God adopts are those who were his enemies; they were guilty rebels; they were under sentence of death. That the children of wrath should be made the heirs of glory is surely an act of astonishing grace!

If we briefly study the privileges which the believer possesses as a result of his adoption by God, we shall see how astonishing God's grace is.

1. Believers now have an honourable character: not servants, not friends, but *children* of God. And this is an unalterable condition. Believers are also called kings and priests.

2. Believers have a remarkable relationship: not merely brothers of Christ, but his bride also. And this is a union never to be dissolved.

3. Believers have an excellent inheritance; not merely all the help of providence in this life, but heirs to all the fulness of God himself.

4. Believers enjoy the benefit of the Spirit of God living in them — the Spirit of adoption — as a guarantee of their future glory and as a practical help to spiritual life now.

What a privilege to be able to come to God without embarrassment or fear. The poorest believer is richer in this respect than all earth's great names.

Now, what do these things mean to *you*? Do you call yourself a Christian? Do you have any experience of the

46

privileges I have spoken of? If not, then, far from being a child of God, you are — how shall I say this? will you accept it? — you are still a child of the devil.

But if you are a believer, you are a child of God. Be careful to behave as such. Let the children of this world satisfy their little minds with earthly things. You should not behave like them. Are you not an heir of the kingdom of God? Then you must care for the welfare of the church of God. "Whatever things are true, whatever things are noble, whatever things are just, whatever things are pure, whatever things are lovely, whatever things are of good report, if there is any virtue and if there is anything praiseworthy — meditate on these things" (Philippians 4:8).

8.
Our sanctification comes by grace

So far I have written about the change that takes place in the way God thinks about those whom he makes his children. His graciously thinks of them now as his chosen children, justified and adopted into his family.

But God not only thinks differently of them, he also graciously makes them *actually different* from what they were before he called them. God calls them while they are ungodly. But he will not allow them to remain ungodly. He graciously gives them a love for himself and his ways. Sanctification is that spiritual process by which those who are justified have the image of God renewed in them. The effect of this is to make them truly holy.

Justification and sanctification both come by God's gracious will. Yet they are different things. Justification is a single act whereby God graciously declares the ungodly person not guilty. Sanctification is a continual process whereby God graciously changes that believer's habits and behaviour into holy deeds. The former frees us from sin's condemnation; the latter frees us from sins's contamination. The former is instantaneous; the latter is progressive.

The persons on whom the blessing of sanctification is bestowed are those who are justified. Holiness is a wonderful blessing of the new covenant, not a condition for our entry into that covenant. Holiness, too, is a gift of God's grace. To explain this more clearly, let me show that only a justified person can do good and holy deeds.

For an act to be a "good deed" in God's sight, it must be done with a right motive, in a right manner and with a right aim; it must be done out of love for God; it must be done in the manner God commands; it must have only God's glory as its aim. No ungodly person can act with the right motive and aim, even if he acts in a right manner.

The good deeds the believer does are not to earn his salvation. He has been given that salvation as a gift of God's grace. But he loves to keep God's laws now out of gratitude and love to this gracious God. So we do not dismiss God's law as irrelevant. Indeed, as Jesus said, "He who has my commandments and keeps them, it is he who loves me" (John 14:21). True obedience comes from love to God; true love is obedient to God.

Holiness in believers is the result of their being united to Christ. The Holy Spirit lives in them because they are united to Christ. And the Spirit uses the Bible to influence believers to produce holiness in heart and life. As Jesus prayed: "Sanctify them by your truth. Your word is truth" (John 17:17). And since the Bible is the basis of faith, the clearer we understand its truth, the more will the fruit of holiness be produced in our lives.

There are certain arguments used in the scripture to urge believers to seek holiness:

1. They are God's elect, or God's purchased, people. Surely the price paid for this people — the precious blood of Jesus — is enough to persuade them to hate sin and love God's law? Christians standing at the foot of the cross and seeing the suffering of the Saviour ought to be eager to oppose all sin. "If anyone does not love the Lord Jesus Christ, let him be accursed" (I Corinthians 16:22).

2. They have a heavenly calling. "As he who called you

is holy, you also be holy in all your conduct" (I Peter 1:15). God has called believers that they should be holy. That will encourage them to be what they ought to be.

3.   God's gracious mercies, especially the mercy of the free pardon of all sin, produce a cheerful obedience to God. "I beseech you therefore, brethren, by the mercies of God, that you present your bodies a living sacrifice, holy, acceptable to God, which is your reasonable service" (Romans 12:1). These mercies, being received, even though undeserved, cause the believer to adore the grace of God.

4.   Believers are adopted by God as sons and heirs. Since the indwelling Holy Spirit can be grieved when any believer behaves in an ungodly way, the believer has a strong inducement not to live carelessly.

5.   The promises of God also urge the child of God to press forward after holiness. "By which have been given to us exceedingly great and precious promises, that through these you may be partakers of the divine nature, having escaped the corruption that is in the world through lust" (II Peter 1:4).

6.   The discipline which God exercises as Father of his children. It is the duty of a careful father to chasten his children when they are disobedient. "Now no chastening seems to be joyful for the present, but grievous; nevertheless, afterwards, it yields the peaceable fruit of righteousness" (Hebrews 12:11). It is a sad thing if believers only seek holiness because they fear God's chastisement; yet it is a reason to persuade us to avoid disobedience, and does arise from God's gracious love.

These are not all the ways in the Bible in which believers are encouraged to be holy, but they are perhaps the principle ways. And they do serve to prove that sanctification is an important part of our salvation. God's grace to sinners is not an excuse for them to remain ungodly. Though holiness does not give them right to eternal life, the children of God should always remember that there is no real evidence they are saved if the fruit of holiness is missing from their lives.

It is also clear that since no deed is acceptable to God except it be done out of true love to him, then even the best deeds of unbelievers are no more than splendid faults! It is preposterous to tell sinners to do this, or that, good thing in order to know Christ as their Saviour. Saving knowledge of Christ is not acquired by the sinner but graciously given by God.

> "Without this, all that you do, however it may please your minds, or ease your consciences, is not at all accepted by God. You run, it may be earnestly; but you run out of the way. You strive, but not lawfully, and shall never receive the crown . . . The foundation of spiritual obedience must be laid in God's grace . . . From hence must works of obedience proceed, if you would find acceptance with God".[1]

So it is the graciousness of what God has done which is the motive for true holiness. Make it your concern, then, believer to have a clear idea of what divine grace is. The same grace which provides, reveals and gives the blessings of salvation, becomes the master who teaches and urges you to walk in holy ways.

9.
The importance of holiness and good deeds

This chapter gives some important reasons why believers must do good deeds. We must insist that the gospel is absolutely free to the worst of sinners — for it is by God's grace — yet, equally, we must also insist that whoever fails to live a holy life cannot be a Christian. Good deeds cannot earn our salvation but they are the evidence of it.

Everyone who has been born from above possesses a new spiritual life. The image of God is restored in believers. Is it possible, then, that such people will not be holy? Two important reasons for holiness and good deeds are:

1. Holiness of life proves the truth of our claims to be God's children. Whoever pretends to believe in Jesus and yet is careless about doing good, has a worthless faith.

2. Good deeds, especially help given to poor and persecuted believers, will be remembered by Jesus at the judgment day. That will be the evidence of those who are truly Christian, distinguishing them from unbelievers and nominal believers.

Observe carefully, however, that doing good is never the reason for our being justified. The righteousness by which we are justified has to be perfect, to pass the divine scrutiny. But our best deeds are imperfect. None of them could justify us!

So we distinguish between the basis of our acceptance with God (which is the righteousness of Christ freely given us), and the superstructure built on that foundation — our own practical godliness.

"Our foundation, in dealing with God, is Christ alone; it is grace and pardon in him. Our building is by holiness and obedience. And some men make great mistakes in this matter, and have no comfort in their faith. The reason is because they will be forever bringing their obedience and duties to the foundation. Such stones are not suitable to carry the whole weight of a building! The only foundation to be laid is grace, mercy and pardon by the blood of Christ. When this is laid, then, all our days we are to build upon it the fruits of our faith".[1]

So holiness and good deeds are essential to our Christian character. To be lacking in practical godliness, while claiming to be Christian, is to be an idolater.

Often, the reason why so-called Christians do not do godly deeds is because they are covetous. This sin is greatly misunderstood. I often hear the remark: "He is a good Christian — but a covetous man". You might as well say: "She is a good women but keeps a brothel". The one statement is no more absurd than the other. Covetousness is not a trifling fault. It is idolatry — a damnable crime (I Corinthians 6:9,10; Ephesians 5:5; Colossians 3:5). Perhaps there are few sins for which so many excuses are made. Consequently there are few sins against which we need to be so on our guard. Covetousness is believing that this life is only for the purpose of getting possessions. "Take heed", said Jesus, "and beware of covetousness, for one's life does not consist in the abundance of the things he possesses" (Luke 12:15).

The person who pretends to have faith in Jesus but doesn't habitually live under the healthy influence of love to God and fellow human beings, has no claim to be a Christian. That is how important good deeds are!

10.
Grace keeps believers safe till they reach heaven

In previous chapters we have seen what wonderful privileges are given to the believer by God's gracious generosity — justification, adoption, sanctification. But any believer who understands the weakness of his own heart and the strength of his spiritual enemies will quickly ask: How do I know that I shan't lose these priceless gifts? Grace has given them; but how shall I retain them? Remember Peter! "Even if all are made to stumble because of you, I will never be made to stumble"..."Even if I have to die with you, I will not deny you!" (Matthew 26:33,35). He spoke so confidently! Yet he failed. How, then, shall we persevere?

The Bible says that God can enable so that even a "worm ... shall thresh the mountains" (Isaiah 41:14,15). Yes, believers *will* persevere. This is not hard to believe when we remember that the Triune God is wholly committed to preserve his children. Here are some reasons for our security.

1. God's *love* will keep believers secure. Having once chosen them by his gracious love, either his love must die or it must be prevented from doing what he wishes, before the believer can be lost. God's love is unchangeable; his purposes cannot be thwarted.

2.   God's *power* will keep believers secure. If one saved soul could be lost, then we would doubt whether God is all-powerful; his glory would be in question; his wisdom would be shown to be incomplete.

3.   The *promises* of God will keep believers secure. God has given many promises to his children, such as "I will never leave you nor forsake you" (Hebrews 13:5). These promises are given to us "in which it is impossible for God to lie" (Hebrews 6:18).

4.   God's *covenant* will ensure the believer is kept secure. The believer is the subject of the new covenant of grace made by Christ. This is a far better agreement than the old covenant made with Adam (which was temporary, giving life only as long as he perfectly obeyed). The new covenant is described as an "everlasting covenant". God says: "I will not turn away from doing them good . . . I will give them one heart and one way, that they may fear me for ever" (Jeremiah 32:39,40). What greater security could there be than a covenant like this?

5.   God's *faithfulness* will keep believers secure. God says: "I will not . . . allow my faithfulness to fail" (Psalm 89:33). Rejoice, then, feeble believer! The basis of your confidence is strong — stronger than the troubles of life; stronger than the fears of death; stronger than the terrors of judgment. The God of power, of truth and of grace is faithful, too!

6.   The value of *Christ's sacrifice,* his intercession for his people and his union with them ensures the believer will be kept. Would he have suffered so much, only to lose those whom he redeemed? If he is responsible to "the Father who sent me, that of all he has given me I should lose nothing" (John 6:39), can we suppose he will fail? Can we think that his prayers will be ignored by the Father who delights in him? If believers are united to him, as members of the spiritual body of which he is the head,

56

how can they be lost?

7. *The Holy Spirit,* living in believers, keeps them secure. He is their guide and strengthens them. His purpose in living in them is to bring them to glory. He is the "guarantee of our inheritance" (Ephesians 1:14). A guarantee like this must ensure that believers reach their future inheritance.

8. *The scriptures* and *church ordinances*[1] are given in order to keep believers secure. The promises, the exhortations, the examples and the warnings in the Bible all combine to guide the believer. Believers have their faith confirmed, their holiness advanced, and their understanding increased by the ordinances of the church.

On the whole, then, we have every reason to agree with Paul that wherever God begins a good work he will certainly complete it (Philippians 1:6). Believers are branches of a vine that never withers; members of a head who never dies; living — not by their own life — but by the life of Christ.

Here, perhaps, there may be objections; i.e. if the preservation of believers depends so much on God, then need they be at all careful how they live, if their final security is guaranteed? This was precisely how Satan tempted our Lord. "If you are the Son of God, throw yourself down . . . he shall give his angels charge concerning you" (Matthew 4:6). Our Lord — who had not the slightest doubt of his Father's care for him — rejected Satan's argument with abhorrence, because it was based on a wrong use of scripture. The believer will react in the same way and refuse to live carelessly. God's promises are not given to permit us to sin more easily. Other arguments can also be used here, but since they have been considered already I will not repeat them.[2]

Nor is it reasonable to argue that since believers are

57

urged to pray for God's help all the time, their final position must be uncertain. Christ himself prayed earnestly and often to his Father. Was Christ's future uncertain? No! Praying for God's help is a sensible thing for believers to do, for if they are careless and disobedient, their heavenly Father must chastise them. When they realise that their backslidings grieve the Spirit, and bring dishonour on God and the gospel, they learn to pray earnestly for help. Prayer is needed for a successful spiritual life now, even though final perseverance *is* certain for the future. True believers cannot be indifferent and careless when untiring spiritual enemies are eager to bring about their downfall.

Yet believers may be comforted, too. God's grace has begun saving them and all that is necessary to make sure they will reach perfection is also graciously provided by God. Happy indeed are those who live in the kingdom of grace.

11.
Grace is successful because of who Christ is

Our salvation is so perfect because Jesus Christ is so unique. We should give careful attention to understanding his natures. Christ had two natures, though he was one person. He was God AND he was a man. The fact that he was unique in this way is the reason why the redemption he obtained and graciously gives to us, is so perfect.

He had to be a real man. God's law was originally given for human beings to keep, so someone must show that a person could keep it successfully. Adam had failed. But Christ succeeded; he never once failed to please his Father. And Christ's law-keeping was acceptable because he was truly human. If he had been an angel, his law-keeping would not have proved that a *man* could keep God's law. It was Adam, a man, who sinned; therefore, Christ, a man must now offer complete obedience. In addition, Christ's human nature must be *related* to that of our first parents. It would not be suitable if his human nature were suddenly created out of nothing, for then he would not be related to those he came to save. The right of redemption belongs only to a near relative (Leviticus 25:48,49).

On the other hand, it is equally important that his human nature should be free from sin. If he had been polluted in the slightest way with that sinfulness which we inherit, then he could no more have kept God's law than we can. How wise God is! Though it was necessary for the Saviour to be born of a woman, yet he was conceived in such a manner as to be free from Adam's guilt (Matthew 1.20). Christ took the nature which had sinned (in Adam) without any of the sinfulness inherent in that nature.

It was also absolutely necessary that the Saviour was God as well as man. We humans have to obey God because we are dependent on him for everything. So our need to obey is because of our dependence. Because we are *totally* dependent on him, we must be *totally* obedient to him. No part of us is independent of God, and so available to obey God on behalf of someone else. Our whole obedience must be for ourselves alone. Only a person with no need to obey God on his own account can obey on behalf of others. Therefore, our Saviour must be God and not dependent on God as we are. Only a divine person who is not dependent on any other person, can do obedient acts unnecessary for himself and so available for others.

Sin is an infinite evil. The badness of any evil deed is measured by the importance of the law that it breaks. And the importance of any law is in proportion to the loveliness and status of the person who makes it. Therefore, since God possesses infinite beauty, status and authority, his laws are of infinite importance and we must be completely obedient to them. Our disobedience is infinitely criminal. Consequently, our sin deserves infinite punishment. So who else could endure the weight of an infinitely divine wrath on infinitely evil sins, except an infinitely divine Saviour? Jesus must be God as well as man, to be an adequate redeemer.

And, lastly, our Saviour must be both man and God *at the same time.* He is to be a mediator between God and man; between the offended sovereign and the offending sinner. If Jesus were only divine, he could not represent people. If Jesus were only human, he could not plead with God. Deity alone was too high for human beings; humanity alone was too low for God. Jesus must be both at once and so be the middle person touching both God and human beings.

For Jesus to carry out his duties as priest, prophet and king, he must be both God and man.

1. As a priest, he must have something to offer (Hebrews 8:3). But pure divinity would not have anything to offer to God. Christ has, therefore, to be a man in order to have a perfect humanity to offer. But as a mere man, he would have no authority to lay down his life and take it up again. Christ had, therefore, to be God in order to possess that authority. He died for infinite sinfulness so the offering of his humanity must have infinite status to be adequate. That status could only come from his divinity.

2. As a prophet, he needed to be God in order to know the mind of God and to understand the variety of those in every age and nation who need his teaching. But in order to reveal God's will in his life by ways suitable for people to grasp, he needed to be a man.

3. As a king, Christ needed to be God in order to be the Lord of our consciences, the head of the church, the giver of eternal life to his followers and the judge of all. Yet he needed also to be a man, for without that, he could not be a head of the same nature as the body to which he is united; nor could he sympathise, as he does, with his subjects.

We may, therefore, have the fullest assurance in the excellence of Christ's work as redeemer, because he is so excellently equipped for it by his unique person with two natures. The salvation that such an excellent Saviour graciously gives must be the best that there can be. Grace reigns!

Here let the reader admire and adore the love and wisdom of God! And note how serious it is to deny that Christ is truly God or that he is truly man. Both errors destroy his excellence as a true mediator between God and believers. Both the deity and the humanity of Christ are essential to a right understanding of all Christ's saving work.

May sinners run to such a suitable Saviour! Trust him as mighty to save; look to him for instruction in truth; expect protection from him as king; yield him obedience; worship him; for he is over all, God blessed for ever. By his excellence, the excellence of God's grace is shown.

12.
Grace is successful because of what Christ has done

We have seen how the excellence of the Saviour makes possible an excellent salvation for us. Now we must see how excellent is the saving work that the Saviour has done. "Grace reigns through righteousness" is how Paul puts it (Romans 5:21). In other words, God's grace comes to us, not because God overlooks the fact that his holy law is broken by us, but because God's law is fully satisfied by Christ's righteous acts on our behalf. In this way, God still honours his holy law and yet can be gracious to those ungodly sinners for whom Christ died.

Let us think about the excellence of what Christ did. His obedience was faultless. He kept God's law exactly. His motive, the manner and the aim of his actions — to glorify God — were always right. He paid precisely whatever God's law required as penalty for our sins. His infinite status as God-man fully satisfied the infinite wrath of God's justice. The righteousness of Christ is as excellent as divine wisdom could devise!

Christ's righteousness is described in the Bible by such pictorial language as fine linen, clean and white; clothing of wrought gold; the best robe; the righteousness of God; an everlasting righteousness. It is said to be completely finished and not something to which we have to add any deeds of ours.

It may be that my readers will readily agree that the righteousness of Christ is indeed as excellent as all this. But they may ask: Is it available for good people only, or for sinners? To this, the Bible insists that Christ's righteousness is not only excellent, everlasting and complete, but is is also free, which means it is exactly suitable for the sinner. We do not have to ascend to heaven to find Christ; nor to descend to the depths; God's grace brings the word of hope down to us (Romans 10:5-9). We do not have to perform any impossible tasks to obtain this splendid righteousness. Grace makes it freely available. What an encouragement this is to the sinner!

Christians of all time have gloried in this righteousness as the only ground of their hope. Who can describe it adequately? As "the righteousness of God" it is better than all possible human praise, as God is indescribably more glorious than a man! God is happy to be gracious to us, when his law has been kept so righteously by Christ on our behalf.

13.
The final purpose of God's grace

God's grace is more wonderful than graciousness among human beings because of the astonishing gifts it brings to undeserving sinners. And the final purpose of God's grace is as glorious as the grace itself. God's final purpose is that sinners should be brought at last to the blissful place of everlasting life with him. Heaven is God's ultimate gracious gift.

The Bible uses pictorial language to describe the happiness of heaven. It speaks of crowns, thrones and a kingdom. It speaks of an everlasting inheritance to be enjoyed by the sons of God. It speaks of pleasures for ever at God's right hand.

Believers already have some foretaste of this joy. Faith is described as the "substance of things hoped for" (Hebrews 11:1). The believer has everlasting life now. Perhaps the joys of the world-to-come are anticipated more clearly at some times than at others, but they will be felt in some measure at all times.

The future happiness of believers may be thought of in two stages — first, after death and before the resurrection; and, second, after the resurrection and the judgment.

1. The believer's soul enters into glory immediately at death. So death, for the believer, is a blessing! "All things are yours", said Paul". . . life or death . . . " (I Corinthians 3:21,22). Death is glory's gate. And, as Paul says elsewhere, we are "well pleased rather to be absent from the body and to be present with the Lord" (II Corinthians 5:8). As Jesus said to the dying thief: "Today you will be with me in paradise" (Luke 23:43). Christ promised him the joys of paradise as soon as death took place.

Completely released from all troubles of every kind, the eternal spirits of the saints enjoy being with Christ. They see his glory and his perfections dazzlingly revealed, which they only dimly understood before. They worship with adoring gratitude the grace that has brought them there.

Nor are they simply looking at the glorious Lord. He is attentive to them and rejoices with them. Surely we may learn this from the friendly relationship he had with his disciples here on earth? He is now exalted in heaven and his friendship with his family in glory must be more exalted, too. They share his glory. And that must increase their astonishment!

The ability of the believer to appreciate the glories of the Saviour's redemption must be greatly increased once the sinful dullness of this world is left behind. And if Paul, with earthly understanding, could excitedly exclaim: "Oh, the depth of the riches both of the wisdom and knowledge of God!" (Romans 11:33), how much greater must be the wonder experienced by the souls of believers in heaven! For there they see the great riches of God with unhindered vision. They see God's power. They see God's love. They see — as never before — the full meaning of what Christ did to save them. They see, in heaven, the full wonder of God's grace to them, unworthy sinners that they were. What ecstasies of delight! What rapturous emotions!

Nor will the sight of divine justice, revealed in wrath on

unbelievers, in the least diminish their pleasure in God. For now their holy wills are so completely at one with the will of God that they fully agree with what he does.

If the face of Moses shone after he had been face to face with God on Mount Sinai, how much greater must be the brilliance which God communicates to those who see him in glory. And seeing God more clearly will mean their love to him will be increased. Free from all selfishness and pride and from all the physical imperfections which spoil worship here below, the saints in heaven can, as never before, adore this God of all grace.

2. But while the experience of heaven is as happy as this to the "unclothed" spirits of believers, it falls short of that happiness which will be theirs after the resurrection.

In the resurrection, the bodies of believers will be raised and re-united with their spirits. That will be joy! As long as the bodies of saints are confined to the grave, the effect of sin is not entirely conquered. But when the body is raised again, made new without sin, and united to the believer's sinless soul, the victory over the damage sin had done is triumphantly complete.

It is a fundamental part of Christian belief that the same bodies which died because of sin shall be raised again to demonstrate Christ's victory over sin. Yet though they are the same bodies, they will be different in nature. The bodies will now be incorruptible, glorious and powerful; they will be spiritual, like the resurrection body of Christ. Who can imagine the splendour of that body? (I Corinthians 15:42-44; I John 3:2).

Another thing that will add to the happiness of the resurrection for the believer is the fact that he will then be publicly acquitted by the judge of all the earth. The judge is Christ, his friend and Saviour. Christ's righteousness protects him. Christ's blood atoned for his sin. Who can condemn him?

And this happiness is for ever. The inheritance is safe from any enemy. The crown is unfading. The kingdom is eternal. The happiness of the believer is as long-lasting as his God who has so favoured him by his grace. And God is infinite.

So it was God's gracious mercy that first conceived the way of salvation and chose those ungodly ones who should receive it. It was God's gracious decision that pardoned, justified, adopted and sanctified his children. It was God's gracious favour which provided all the necessary blessings to nurture and preserve the spiritual life of believers. And finally, it is God's gracious willingness that opens heaven to believers as an eternal home. God's grace has been central from first to last. When the whole story is finished, what rejoicing there will be in heaven "with shouts of grace, grace unto it" (Zechariah 4:7). And all the angels will shout for joy, too.

What other things will add to the happiness of believers in heaven? I will not presume to enquire. We should not indulge in curious imagination. The important thing for us to know is that we are heirs of this joy.

Reader, what are your thoughts about all this? Probably you hope to go to heaven when you die. Is that a mere wish, or a well-grounded hope? Why do *you* hope to be happy when many will be eternally miserable? Only those who know God's grace on earth will see his glory in heaven. You can have no genuine hope of heaven in the future if you have no love of holiness now, for heaven, were you there, would not be a happy place for you! If you do not love heaven but are merely afraid of hell, may God's grace deliver you, for at present you are an heir of destruction. If you leave this world in such a condition, that is how you will be eternally.

Are you a serious person? Do you base your hope on your seriousness? A person may be zealous for God and yet perish for ever (Romans 9:31). If you truly love your soul, do not be uncertain about its future. Read your Bible; pray that the Spirit of truth may direct you.

Are you a child of God? Then try to make swift progress in vital religion. Use all the means of grace. Maintain regular communion with God. Guard against indwelling sin. Never forget that apart from Christ and God's grace you are an unworthy, guilty, creature. Always behave in such a way that when your heavenly Bridegroom comes again, he may find you ready.

Perhaps now we have learnt that the free favour of God shown to us in salvation by grace is a theme so sublime that all that might be said, or written, must fall short of a full study of it. Yes! the subject will remain unexhausted even in eternity, for the riches of Christ are unsearchable and the grace of God is unbounded.

References

Preface

1. i.e. those who have been spiritually awakened to a knowledge of their sinful *state* in God's sight. – Ed.

Introduction

1. i.e. a person who, by the Holy Spirit, has been made aware of his sinnership. – Ed.

Chapter 3.

1. This is a very long chapter in Abraham Booth's book. As he explains in his preface, he at one time opposed this truth. He now writes fully to explain it. We have, therefore, in this easy-to-read edition, divided the chapter into two parts. – Ed.

Chapter 4.

1. Let no-one suppose that the description I have given of the experience of sinners being awakened by the Spirit to their spiritual needs is a precise standard to which every believer must come. Every sinner must feel his want before he will apply for grace. But God has many different ways to make his people willing. The vital question is not, How much conviction have I now? but rather, Do I truly know that I have sinned and deserve to perish? – A. Booth

Chapter 5.

1. We have altered A. Booth's order (which was "full, free and everlasting") in order to stress the graciousness of it, since this is the theme of this book. – Ed.

2. How amazing are the ways of grace! During his life, Jesus was approached by a very decent and devout young ruler seeking eternal life by conditions he thought he had fulfilled, but who "went away sorrowful". Here, however, Jesus gives pardon to the first prayer of an undeserving wretch. – A. Booth

3. Abraham Booth quotes this paragraph from John Owen's writing on Psalm 130 — "A practical exposition of the nature of forgiveness of sin". – Ed.

Chapter 6.

1. Abraham Booth comments in a footnote: Though I write of our pardon and our justification in two separate chapters, they are blessings which cannot really be separated. He who is pardoned is justified, and vice versa. Yet there are differences. A person who is pardoned is still considered as one who had transgressed. But when a person is justified, he is considered as righteous. Pardon only means punishment waived; justification means reward is deserved!

2. This paragraph is quoted from John Owen's writing "On Justification", chapter 18. – Ed.

3. Here Abraham Booth has a section dealing with the idea, prevalent in his day, that Christ's dying has brought to an end the old law and that we now have only to keep an easier law of Christ and can earn our justification, even by an imperfect obedience. He argues that the idea of imperfect obedience is absurd because any law is meant to be kept and to break it is sin. God, who requires perfection, cannot therefore justify any on the grounds of an imperfect obedience because that is sin! – Ed.

Chapter 8.

1. This paragraph is quoted from John Owen's writing on Psalm 130. – Ed.

Chapter 9.

1. Abraham Booth quotes this paragraph from John Owen's writing on Psalm 130. – Ed.

Chapter 10.

1. By this phrase, Abraham Booth means the preaching of scripture truth, baptism and the Lord's Supper. – Ed.
2. See Chapter 3, Part II and Chapter 9. – Ed.

SOME OTHER
GRACE PUBLICATIONS TRUST TITLES

GREAT CHRISTIAN CLASSICS

No. 1 Life by His Death!
An easier-to-read and abridged version of the classic "The Death of Death in the Death of Christ" by John Owen, first published in 1647.
Paperback, 100 pages, £1.50

". . . a brilliant abridgement of that wonderful book. The whole church of Christ stands in debt to John Appleby for undertaking this work. It will open the door into Owen's volume for countless believers who might otherwise miss its treasures." Evangelical Times.

No. 2 God Willing
An easier-to-read and abridged version of the classic "Divine Conduct or the Mystery of Providence" by John Flavel, first published in 1677.
Paperback, 78 pages, £1.50

No. 3 Biblical Christianity
An easier-to-read and abridged version of the classic "Institutes of the Christian Religion" by John Calvin, first published in 1536.
John Calvin's "Institutes of the Christian Religion" is perhaps the finest summary of Christian truth since the apostles, yet its very size and comprehensiveness has been a stumbling block to many. Biblical Christianity, written as an easier-to-read and abridged version, offers an ideal introduction to a work with which every Christian should be familiar.
Paperback, 125 pages, £1.95

GRACE GATEWAY BOOKS

Introductions to Great Christian Writings

1. WHO IS IN CONTROL?
An easy-to-read version of the substance of "The Sovereignty of God" by A. W. Pink, prepared by Roger Devenish.
Paperback, 60 pages, £1.20.

2. INTO LIFE
An easy-to-read version of the substance of "The Rise and Progress of Religion in the Soul" by Philip Doddridge, prepared by Roger Devenish.
Paperback, 60 pages, £1.20.

Other titles in course of preparation include:

"THE BEST THAT WE CAN BE" from William Law's "Serious Call to a Devout and Holy Life".

"WHAT'S THE GOOD OF IT?" from A. W. Pink's "Profiting from the Word".

"WHAT'S REAL?" from Gardiner Spring's "Distinguishing Traits of Christian Character".

A full list of Books, Work-books, Booklets and Tracts published by

GRACE PUBLICATIONS TRUST
(including "Grace Hymns")

may be obtained from the Secretary

Grace Publications Trust,
139 Grosvenor Avenue,
London, N5 2NH.